7 Mindsets to Success

The generator of every success

By
Teddy J. Beasley

Disclaimer

The information in this book is just meant to be generally informative. The author and publisher make no claims or guarantees about the accuracy, timeliness, or completeness of the information. It is advised that readers look for specialized help from experts who can best handle their individual situation. The writer or publisher disclaims all liability for any injury or loss arising from the use of this book.

About the author

University of California, Berkeley alumnus Teddy J. Beasly is an American novelist and professor. In Teddy's nine global blockbusters on success and strategy, "7 mindsets to success" is the fourth.

Table of contents

The mindset of a champion
The mindset of a fighter
Mindset of discipline
Mindset of persistence
A mindset of patience
Mindset of never giving up

Introduction

In a world continuously seeking the elusive formula for success, this book emerges as a glow of understanding and clarity. This compilation is not merely a list of theories; rather, it is the result of a careful examination, perceptive analysis, and real-world applications that were condensed into seven essential mindsets. These kinds of thinking are more than just paths; they are the fundamental engine that propels the pursuit of achievement in all facets of life. As you read these pages, get ready to go on a life-changing journey where you will discover the fundamental ideas that have helped countless people and organizations all over the world realize their full potential. From leadership to entrepreneurship, personal growth, and leadership to creativity, this book is your companion, revealing the route to success with each turn of the page. Through fascinating narratives, strong methods, and concrete activities, it equips you with the

mental tools necessary to handle challenges, take opportunities, and create a mindset poised for continuous success. Join us on this adventure into the core of achievement, where the seven mindsets merge to become not merely a guide but the very generator of your achievements.

Mindset of believing

The acceptance of anything as true or real, usually in the absence of evidence, is referred to as belief. Belief influences how people view the world and might be based on personal, religious, or philosophical ideas. Beliefs have the power to shape actions, choices, and interpersonal relationships. Generally speaking, belief systems can also impact cultures, communities, and even global events.

A mindset of believing comprises a deep-seated conviction in specific concepts, ideas, or ideals. This mindset involves sustaining faith in the validity of these beliefs, often despite obstacles or contradicting information. It can also involve a readiness to act in accordance with these views and to defend or promote them to others.

A mindset of belief can be important in forming one's worldview, influencing activities, and generating a sense of purpose and identity. It can also affect how individuals engage with others and the world around them.

A mindset of belief can substantially contribute to your achievement. When you fully believe in your abilities, ambitions, and the likelihood of reaching achievement, it can lead to various favorable outcomes.

Believing in yourself and your goals can build resilience in the face of adversity. Individuals with a strong belief attitude are more inclined to endure setbacks and disappointments, perceiving them as transitory difficulties rather than insurmountable roadblocks.

Believing in your skills
can serve as a powerful
motivator, encouraging
you to take initiative and
follow your dreams with
perseverance and passion.
This proactive approach
generally leads to more
chances and results.
An attitude of believing
instills confidence, which
can favorably impact how
you present yourself,
interact, and engage with
others. Confidence can
attract support,
collaboration, and
chances that contribute to
success.
Belief in the attainability
of your goals drives you
to set ambitious yet
reasonable objectives and
work persistently towards
them. This focused effort
increases the likelihood

of reaching the desired
goals.
A strong belief attitude
can embolden you to take
calculated chances and
explore unique ideas.
This willingness to move
outside of your comfort
zone often leads to
breakthroughs and new
prospects for
achievement.
Individuals with a
mindset of believing can
inspire and influence
others with their
conviction and passion.
This can lead to
leadership chances and
the ability to mobilize
support for common
aims.
Believing in yourself and
your journey may foster a
good mentality and
emotional well-being,

which are vital for managing hurdles and sustaining focus on long-term success.

It fosters the motivation needed to overcome difficulties and endure in the face of challenges.

Without belief, it might be difficult to retain the energy and determination essential to achieving success.

Belief develops a positive mindset, which can lead to improved confidence, inventiveness, and a willingness to take chances.

A positive outlook is typically a vital aspect of obtaining success.

Belief can impact behavior and actions.

When individuals believe in their ability to succeed,

they are more inclined to
take proactive measures,
pursue their objectives,
look for chances, and
persevere in the midst of
difficulty.
Occasionally, it turns into
a self-fulfilling prophecy.
People are more inclined
to take action when they
have confidence in their
potential to succeed,
which leads to behaviors
that lead to success,
establishing a reinforcing
cycle of belief and
achievement.
This approach helps you
achieve your objectives
and make meaningful
contributions to both your
career and personal life.
Unquestionably, having
faith is a strong mentality
that can help one succeed,
particularly when faced

with difficulties and misfortune. But it's equally important to combine action, preparation, and critical thought with conviction. It's not always the case that believing alone, without making conscious efforts to succeed, produces the desired results. Therefore, to maximize the possibility of achievement, while belief is essential, it should be paired with wise planning and execution.

Mindset of a champion

A champion is someone who has achieved tremendous achievement or victory in a

competition, sport, or any other effort. It can also apply to someone who strongly argues for a subject or speaks up for others. The term "champion" is generally connected with excellence, leadership, and a strong sense of success.
The attitude of a champion often incorporates a combination of drive, resilience, focus, and a strong belief in oneself. Champions frequently exhibit a strong will to succeed, a willingness to push through difficulties and disappointments, and a commitment to constant growth. They are able to retain a positive attitude, stay motivated, and

remain focused on their goals, even in the face of hardship. Additionally, champions frequently display a great level of discipline, mental toughness, and a desire to learn from both achievements and setbacks. Overall, the attitude of a champion is characterized by a strong sense of purpose, steadfast determination, and a tireless pursuit of perfection.

In the face of setbacks, champions are resilient. They view obstacles as chances for development and education rather than insurmountable hurdles. People with this resilience are able to push through difficult

circumstances and keep
pursuing their objectives.
The mindset of a
champion is marked by
persistent commitment
and focus. Even in the
face of distractions, they
are likely to have a clear
understanding of their
objectives and remain
committed to achieving
them.
Champions frequently
keep a cheerful attitude,
which may be infectious
and inspire those around
them. This positivism can
help individuals negotiate
challenging situations
with grace and discover
solutions to issues more
successfully.
Champions are
committed to ongoing
progress and growth.
They are continually

seeking ways to develop their abilities.
their performance, understanding, and ability to keep one step ahead of their opponents and adjust to changing circumstances. Establishing specific, attainable goals and maintaining the self-control to continually strive toward them are characteristics of a champion's mindset. This strategy aids people in maintaining their motivation, organization, and goal-focusedness. Champions understand the advantages of collaboration and leadership. They have the ability to uplift and encourage people, in addition to

communicating
successfully with a team
to accomplish collective
achievement.
A champion's mindset is
distinguished by mental
tenacity, which allows
individuals to maintain
strength and
concentration under
pressure. People who are
resilient are able to give
their best effort,
particularly when there is
a lot on the line.
They firmly believe in
their own skills and
chances of success.
Self-belief is an essential
component of a
champion's mentality.
Without self-assurance
and faith, it's difficult to
follow big dreams and get
past the uncertainties and
critiques that typically

accompany the route to
success.
This self-confidence
encourages people to take
chances.
Champions are versatile
and receptive to change.
They can alter their
strategies and techniques
as needed, responding
successfully to new
problems and
possibilities.
When you create the
attitude of a champion, it
will foster a combination
of attributes that are
crucial for achieving
success in different
undertakings, including
sports, business,
academics, and personal
growth.
Ultimately, the most
important thing is to build
a mindset that inspires

you to pursue your goals
with enthusiasm and
determination.
Cultivating the mindset of
a champion is vital for
achieving success
because it gives the
mental and emotional
fortitude necessary to
overcome challenges,
stay focused on goals,
and keep a positive and
determined attitude
throughout the route to
achievement. It's the
champion's mindset that
pushes individuals to
overcome challenges,
stay focused on their
goals, push beyond their
limits, learn from failures,
and finally realize their
aspirations.

The mindset of a fighter

The mindset of a fighter is a significant factor that separates them from ordinary people. It covers a combination of cerebral, emotional, and psychological traits that enable warriors to flourish in their chosen sector. Fighters possess unshakeable determination and exceptional perseverance. They are committed to pushing their limitations, conquering challenges, and continually seeking progress. Regardless of failures, they keep focused on their goals and maintain a tireless work ethic.

Fighters develop a high
level of mental toughness
to handle the demands
and trials of their chosen
combat sport. They
exhibit an ability to cope
with stress, adversity, and
pain. They retain a strong
mindset even when facing
intimidating opponents or
when the odds are against
them.
Fighters display
enormous discipline in
training, food, and
lifestyle. They stick to
tight routines and plans,
forsaking momentary
gratification for long-
term success. Their
willpower permits people
to resist temptations and
stay committed to their
goals, especially when
faced with distractions.

Fighters have a great
desire to compete and
win. They thrive on
difficulties and utilize
competition as a source
of motivation. They
always seek progress and
are driven by the desire to
exceed their opponents.
Combatants must be able
to focus under pressure
and maintain their
attention. They
experience a tremendous
deal of mental clarity,
which aids in their ability
to react quickly to the
acts of their opponent and
plot wisely throughout
fights.
Fighters have a great
sense of confidence in
themselves. They have
faith in their skills and are
assured of their
preparation, methods, and

approaches. This self-assurance helps fighters retain composure, make quick judgments, and execute to the best of their skills.

They are continually learning, adapting, and altering their techniques based on the advantages and disadvantages of their opponents. Fighters can maintain their flexibility and competitiveness by adjusting to a variety of styles and situations. Fighters are aware that failure is a necessary step on the path to success. They develop resilience by overcoming setbacks and growing from their errors. Rather than dwelling on failures, they see them as chances to do better and stronger and develop their talents. Visualization plays a key role in a fighter's attitude. They envisage success, imagining themselves excelling at the highest level. By mentally rehearsing their techniques, plans, and desired outcomes, fighters boost their attention and confidence. Above all, fighters display a real love and passion for their chosen combat sport. Their perspective is fueled by their deep attachment to the sport, which drives their dedication and quest for excellence.

Understand that the mindset of a fighter is a complicated blend of drive, mental toughness,

discipline, competition,
focus, self-confidence,
flexibility, resilience,
visualization, and a
genuine passion for their
craft. These traits enable
them to meet obstacles
head-on and perform at
their best, both inside and
outside the ring or
octagon.

Mindset of discipline

The mindset of discipline
is a state of mind that
focuses on structure,
consistency, and self-
control. It is the
willingness to undertake
what is hard and difficult
in the present moment for
long-term advantages and
achievements. A
disciplined mentality is
all about taking

responsibility for your decisions and actions and establishing the focus and perseverance to persevere with your goals despite challenges and disappointments. A disciplined mentality requires defining clear, defined, and quantifiable goals, planning your activities in advance, and following through continuously with the acts needed to attain your goals. This involves putting what is important first and sacrificing quick gratification for long-term gains. Such a mindset requires creating habits and routines that correspond with your goals and beliefs, such as time management, frequent exercise, and good eating. Discipline also includes being responsible for your actions, holding yourself responsible for your faults, and making corrections when necessary. A disciplined attitude calls for conquering fear, procrastination, and lack of confidence by creating resilience, tenacity, and perseverance. It involves focusing on what you can manage, retaining a good attitude, and exercising self-reflection to find areas for growth and change. In summary, a disciplined attitude is all about having clear goals, planning and taking continuous action, being responsible for them, sacrificing short-term pleasures, and cultivating endurance to overcome problems and achieve long-term success.

Mindset of persistence

Having an attitude of tenacity can actually lead to success and prosperity in several facets of life. A tenacious mindset encourages individuals to endure through hurdles and setbacks. Instead of giving up easily, they keep their concentration, passion, and tenacity. This enables them to identify other solutions, learn from failures, and ultimately achieve the objectives they set. They understand that success often requires

continual effort and
change. They have the
resilience to keep
learning, adjusting, and
polishing their talents.
This commitment to
developing themselves
boosts their skills and
raises their chances of
achieving long-term
success.
Success and money often
come from becoming
particularly skilled or
educated in a certain
sector. A tenacious
mindset motivates
individuals to spend time
and effort developing
their craft. By regularly
practicing, receiving
criticism, and striving for
greatness, they establish a
profound competence that
sets them apart from
others.

Consistent individuals are more likely to notice and take advantage of opportunities. They actively search out fresh possibilities, network with relevant individuals, and take measured risks. Their determination motivates them to push beyond their comfort zones and embrace possible paths for success and wealth development. Persistence is intimately tied to having a long-term perspective. Rather than seeking quick gratification, tenacious individuals are willing to delay immediate benefits in pursuit of larger accomplishments. They set high goals, break them down into achievable steps, and work methodically towards their achievement.

It's crucial to highlight that while tenacity is valuable, it should be accompanied by adaptation, learning from failure, and maintaining a healthy work-life balance. Persistence alone may not ensure success or money, but when combined with other desirable traits, it can considerably raise the likelihood of reaching desired goals.

A mindset of patience

In general terms, patience can be defined as the ability to stay cool and composed in the face of problems, delays, or tough circumstances. It requires suppressing

impatience, annoyance,
or fury while preserving
tenacity and a long-term
perspective.
Patience usually has to do
with waiting without
anxiety. or grievance
when things don't go as
expected. It means
acknowledging that
certain processes or
outputs require time and
understanding that
hurrying or forcing
results may lead to
inferior outcomes.
Furthermore, patience
comprises empathy and
compassion toward
others, allowing space for
their development,
studying, and decision-
making processes. It
requires listening intently,
accepting differing
opinions, and realizing

the significance of collaboration and teamwork.

Cultivating patience can have several benefits, such as reducing stress and anxiety, boosting problem-solving skills, establishing stronger relationships, and supporting personal growth. However, it's vital to highlight that patience doesn't indicate passivity or inaction; rather, it fosters a balanced approach that combines dedication with adaptation and intelligent decision-making. Ultimately, practicing patience can lead to emotional well-being, toughness, and general competence in managing various facets of life.

A mindset of patience
certainly contributes to
both success and wealth.
Here's an overview of
how this quality might
favorably impact
numerous elements of
life:
Patience encourages
individuals to pause,
assess possibilities, and
make well-considered
judgments rather than
acting impulsively. This
leads to better decisions
in investments,
businesses, or
professional pathways,
leading to improved odds
of success and wealth
creation.
This perspective allows
individuals to persevere
through trials,
disappointments, and
failures. Success

generally demands long-term dedication and work. By keeping patience, individuals are more likely to persist in their activities, learn from failures, modify techniques, and ultimately achieve their goals.

A patient mindset permits individuals to defer instant gratification for a higher benefit in the future. This applies to conserving money, investing intelligently, and creating wealth over time. Patiently sticking to financial objectives and avoiding hasty expenditure can lead to long-term financial stability and increased wealth.

Patience is needed for continual learning and skill-building. Success frequently includes gaining new insight and developing skills, which take time and effort. With patience, individuals can negotiate the learning curve, develop essential abilities, and position themselves for chances that can lead to success and financial rewards.

It plays a critical role in fostering meaningful connections with people. Developing solid professional networks, partnerships, and connections with customers requires time and effort. Patience helps individuals build these connections, establishing trust, collaboration, and

possibilities that can contribute to success and prosperity.
A mindset of patience supports thoughtful decision-making, tenacity, delayed gratification, personal growth, and fostering connections. These skills establish a firm foundation for success and can pave the way for financial success and overall fulfillment.

Mindset of never giving up

Having a mindset of never giving up might indeed be essential to gaining success or money.
When faced with challenges or

disappointments, a never-give-up mindset helps individuals continue and push through difficult circumstances. Rather than giving in to failure, they keep their commitment and continue working towards their goals. This dedication allows them to learn from their failures, adapt techniques, and eventually find answers. Success frequently demands rebounding from failures and disappointments. A never-give-up mentality builds resilience, allowing individuals to recover swiftly from setbacks and remain focused on their long-term objectives. By perceiving problems as transitory hurdles rather than impractical barriers, students build mental strength and adaptability. Embracing a never-give-up mentality develops a growth mindset, emphasizing the concept that abilities and intelligence can be developed through devotion and hard work. This mindset pushes individuals to always seek knowledge, gain new abilities, and improve themselves. It enables students to become continuous learners who are open to opinions and eager to enhance their capabilities. People with a never-give-up mindset tend to maintain an optimistic outlook and are more likely to recognize chances where others may only see hurdles. They tackle difficulties with a mentality of possibility and ingenuity, aggressively seeking novel solutions. This thinking permits individuals to find and take advantage of opportunities that could result in success or fortune.

Achieving major success frequently means taking chances and suffering failure along the way. People with a mindset of never giving up consider failing as an initial step toward success rather than an ending. They use setbacks as experiences of learning, adjusting their method, and

persevering until they
attain their intended
goals.

In essence, a mindset of
never giving up develops
tenacity, resilience,
constant learning,
awareness of
opportunities, and
diligence in the face of
failure. By embracing
these attributes,
individuals boost their
chances of earning
success and potentially
developing riches in
numerous aspects of life.